CHRISTIAN POETRY

VOLUME I

About the Translation

This book has made first in the Portuguese language, and the translation was done by myself, based on my knowledge of the English language.

It was not possible to have a consultancy on the correct use of words and expressions of the English language. I apologize if I used something wrong, and I am on hand to make corrections.

Some of the poems had some changes compared to the original in Portuguese. But the changes do not influence the sense. The changes are just for the rhymes and metrics.

About the Book

The poems were inspired by God and are to show his glory. These were written between 2014 and 2015.

There are presented diverse themes, such as family, personal life, daily life, salvation, eternal life, narratives of biblical histories, etc.

Words of the Cross

Adore
Christ
Cross
Eternal life
Faith
Fight
Follow
Glory
God
Grace
Hear
Help
Holy Spirit
Hope
Jesus
Light
Live
Lord
Love
New life
Peace
Poetry
Prayer
Reign
Renovation
Rhyme
Save
Strength
Text
Union
Way
Win
Words

Table of contents

Liberation Came From the Lord

By a perverse pharaoh, they were enslaved,
He only fed them with crumbs and dust.
All of them were massacred.
For the Egyptians, they made statues,
In hard work, they were forced.

The Lord has changed that story,
With Moses and Aaron, He made a covenant.
Talking to them about good liberty,
Ridding them of slavery and torment.

Many have believed in their words and followed them,
Moses spoke to the pharaoh the word of the Lord,
Begging for the liberty of their people,
But, the heart of the pharaoh has hardened.
The much-dreamed departure has not happened.

In that land, God made signals and wonders,
Even so, the pharaoh did not believe.
He had magicians and many things they did.

Then, a big plague, God sent,

Killing all firstborns of the whole land,

Ridding only the Hebrews of this evil.

After that, the pharaoh feared them,

The late and dreamed departure, he gave them.

The Hebrews were getting out of Egypt,

They were almost out, but a pursuit started,

Many chariots and riders were going to them.

The Lord freed them again,

Opening the sea for them to pass through,

All sons of Israel have passed.

When in the sea, the Egyptians entered,

Then, by the Lord, the sea was closed.

All riders, they have seen die in the sea.

One great deliverance like that, only the Lord gives.

Christ

One day, we walked spread.

Each one followed its way.

There was no help or company.

Following alone; it was a sad destiny.

Even being disunited, many had hope.

Waiting for something new and renewed.

The faith kept them firm and safe.

For a new alliance, they were waiting,

That One who would come from the Lord.

At the right time, He came,

Many people recognized and loved Him.

But others just despised Him.

They did not believe in his wonders and signals,

And they even tried to catch Him in many traps.

But what strength does the man have against the Lord?

What can do against the Lord a man full of sins?

They could not do anything to stop Him.

Jesus walked, healed, taught, and rescued.

The faith of his disciples was increased.

Among those who believe, one failed.

For a bit of money, his Lord, he delivered.

The Just One, the Son of Man was oppressed!

Like one innocent sheep, to the slaughter, He was led.

He received a terrible and painful punishment there.

Over Him, there was no condemnation.

His judges did not find any guilt in his accusations.

But "wise people" did not accept,

They led him to be crucified.

On that cross were paid the sins,

My, yours, and of all of us.

With extreme sacrifice, the debt was paid.

The souls of poor sinners were saved.

After the pain and suffering, He has expired.

At that moment, something great happened.

The earth shook, and the curtain of the temple was torn,

In all places had restlessness,

The sky had darkened.

For that one who died, there was much weeping.

After three days, God rescued Him.

By the angels, the stone was rolled,

The only and beloved son, God, resurrected.

For his people, He showed himself, and He was acknowledged,

Then, the faithful people saw the power of God.

The victory over death, Jesus got.

The First Sins

Through you, everything was done,

Everything was created.

Then, a perfect world was made.

In this world, the Lord did the man dwells.

The man was alone.

God gave him a companion,

She was made from the first powder.

The man must love and care for her.

For them together to prosper.

But amid the heaven, there was an intruder,

By one snake with cheating words, they were seduced,

They sinned against the Lord and feared.

God soon discovered, and from heaven, they were expelled.

They were expelled from heaven and came to Earth.

They came to a world, where there is hunger and conflict.

The first battle was in its family,

The life of Abel was taken by Cain.

He killed him and tried to hide.

But the Sovereign Lord knows everything.

Cain was cursed, and his land did not produce anything.

He moved away from the Lord.

For the rest of his life, he continued fleeing.

The Power of God

All kings have been constituted by Thee,

All authorities came from Thee.

The power they have comes from the Lord,

All things they did were authorized by God.

Only the Lord can change something,

His immense power and strength can change everything.

The man is only an instrument,

To make all God's plans.

The hand of God is governing everything,

God allows man to change things.

From humans come commands to take action,

But to the Sovereign Lord belongs the execution.

I recognize that only God can do everything,

In the world, only the Lord commands all things.

Everything that may happen,

I know that is God and his power.

Dwelling Place Among Us

The Lord is in high skies.

He is observing everyone with his omnipresent eyes.

He can hear everyone with his omniscient ears.

By the Holy Spirit, in every place, He is.

We always desire to get closer to Thee,

One dwelling place for you, we built.

It is a temple that we did here.

Then, our prayer will reach your ears.

Besides praying, we always will praise.

Beautiful songs that the Lord gave us.

Songs of adoration and thanksgiving.

So, we do forever to glorify you.

Only your glory can fulfill us,

We stay fulfilled by the Holy Spirit.

That consoles, snuggles, and comforts us,

That One who brings true and eternal peace.

Sacrifice and Regretting

One day, a great sacrifice was made,
Through Jesus Christ, our sins were paid.
As proof of his big and perfect love.

God loved us so much,
He gave his only Son to save us,
He hoped that after his coming,
All people would adore and love Him.

The people forgot the sacrifice.
The people forgot this,
They are practicing all kinds of badness,
They are delivered to wickedness.

They need to believe again in the cross,
Remembering the suffering of our Lord.
To think about the value of what He did.
To understand that only Jesus is the Savior.

In this way, God may forgive everyone,
All horrible sins, He will erase,
All souls who confess the Lord Jesus,
The Lord God will save through his love.

The Rich Man and the Poor Man

We wake up and see many wrong things,
There are sins in everything.
They forgot That One who was crucified for us.
They only want to gain more power.

In another world, power has no value.
Try to buy the devil!
He will laugh a lot at you, and he will say:
"You had the chance to regret your ways,
But you preferred to seek power."

At that time, it will be late,
Money, you no longer appreciate it.
You only have weeping and teeth-gnashing.
In your whole life,
Does money make you satisfied?

You see the man you have humiliated,
He has peace with God in heaven.
In his place, you would like to be.
In life, it was the contrary, what irony!
The poor man would like to be rich.
In death, the rich man wants to be saved.

Keep calm, everyone is dead.

The humble one went to God.

Only the punishment for sins is what you have.

The Lord Hears Me

Lord, I want to follow you every day.

I want to follow the true ways.

Help me God to be free from evils,

I want to be free of all my vanities.

I desire to have full and true praise,

Staying in the spirit of worship and prayer.

To feel your presence the whole time,

Feeling all time your Holy Spirit.

I want to be under your cloak covering.

God! May my voice be heard by the Lord,

May my prayers lift to your throne.

And your ears are attentive for my supplication.

And your hand comes to be my salvation.

Thank you, Lord, for always giving attention to me,

Thank you, God, for all the blessings received.

May my prayer reach the Lord every day,

And your protection and love never go away.

The Strength of the Prophet of the Lord

Oh Lord, how marvelous you are!

You are the unique and true God.

The unique person who can do everything.

All evils, you ever will win.

Your word is true and faithful.

No one can contest you.

Some people even wished to challenge you.

But only the Lord will prevail forever.

One day your prophet was challenged.

Against him came four hundred men.

Those men could not do anything.

Because the Lord made him win.

It came over them divine fire and much power.

Those men were thrown to the ground,

The sword came over them, and their bodies were exposed.

Then, they could not do wicked things.

The holy nation no longer was led by their sins.

The Change That Came From God

We were poor and sinners,

We were guided by other leaders.

We were seeking other beliefs.

We were not concerned about harm and pain.

For much time we walked in the wrong way.

If God was here, we would have gone away.

We were following strange and useless things.

We were seeking futility and vanity.

Even so, the Lord has loved us,

One change in our life, He decreed.

To transform us came his Holy Spirit.

Our troubled lives began to be fixed.

Little by little, our lives were changing,

In new persons, we were converting.

What was old and dirty went away,

One new person with a new desire was generated.

It is born a converted to the Lord,

Fruit of true and pure love.

One strong love that could rescue me,

One great love that can save my soul.

Your Protection

When I wake up, your presence, I can feel.

I open my eyes, breath, and wake up.

There is a breath of life on me.

I am alive, and I thank only Thee.

The Lord is my friend and protector,

He put his shield on me,

Of the destructor and the evils, He is ridding me.

I trust in your ways and decrees,

I seek to follow your holy word,

And learn about the Lord.

I am getting away from the wickedness of the world.

In this terrible world, only the Lord can help.

Because there are too many things against me,

Many evils want to rise,

But the Lord is with me to save me.

From everything bad, He will rid me.

Obedience

The Lord is always teaching us,

He is always showing the way to follow.

He speaks the way we shall go,

One way free from all evils.

His path is good and pleasant,

It is a straight road without detours.

There are some battles and difficulties,

But God is with us, and He helps us.

To follow this path is easy,

It is enough to praise, obey, and worship.

Doing this, He will have mercy on you,

And He will always help and protect you.

Better than his protection, there is no one.

We have to be obedient and grateful.

Then, God will please about me and you,

He will help us with pleasure.

The Creation and the Destruction

The Lord has created everything,

From the little beings to the wild beasts.

He did everything, but among all, He made one special,

The human being who is above others, and he is exceptional.

The human being was done to praise and adore.

In the beginning, it was like that, but after some time, no more.

The human being lost himself and committed many sins.

Bringing suffering to That One who created him.

The Earth was dominated by a multitude of sins,

God was angry about what humans did against Him.

The Lord thought to put to end everything,

He would exterminate all human beings.

Before making everything, someone pleased the Lord,

Noah and his family were loved by God.

God had compassion, and He decided to save them.

One ark, God has ordered to do,

Because a great storm would come to the world.

They could survive only with the ark.

According to the order of the Lord, Noah has built,

He put all the animals and his family.

Then came the storm of the Lord, and there was great fury.

All the world was devastated, and nothing remained.

After the flood, the rains stopped.

Noah and his family got out, and they adored God,

One new life on Earth, they began.

The Dwelling Place of the Lord

Who are we before you, Lord?

What are our lives, if not a vapor?

Even so, in us, the Lord rejoiced.

In a chosen house, He inhabited.

It is a house of praise and adoration.

We go there to supplicate his unction.

One place to speak with the Lord.

To get closer to his love.

When we are lost, we go to seek you,

The Lord hears us, and good things He will do.

When we sin, we go to ask forgiveness.

The Lord comes to us, and He gives his blessings.

Only the true God can hear us,

Only God will stay every time with us.

Because great is his benignity,

And his blessings are for eternity.

The Help of God

One day, I was in great anguish.

Thinking, *Who will help me?*

Who will come to save me?

Then, the answer came to me:

"My son, trust, because the Lord is with you."

In my Lord and my God, I trusted,

In my life, I allowed Him to act.

He acted magnificently.

All my days, God is saving me.

The hand of God was with me,

Protecting me, blessing me, ridding me.

When appeared some enemy,

The Lord was with me and protected me.

Sacrifices

We often make you a request,

We ask for your help to get something.

We go with supplication, praise, and adoration.

The Lord hears us, and He is attentive to our aspirations.

Your ears hear our supplications and moans.

Our heart connects to the Lord,

Waiting for his blessing,

And for a pleasant reply from Him.

For the Lord to grant our wish,

It is necessary to trust in Him.

And some sacrifices may be necessary,

For reaching his grace.

The sacrifice must be with pleasure and happiness.

Then the Lord will stay very glad.

And He will give us the dreamed blessing.

Sinner

I am a poor sinner.

Of your grace, I am not worthy.

Many mistakes and transgressions, I did.

Your affection, I am not worthy of feeling it.

Even so, the Lord loved me,

Ridding me of a terrible destiny.

The Lord came and introduced himself to me.

Your word has changed my life.

The Lord is a God so marvelous,

He has rid my spirit of a terrible end.

Your hand came to rescue me,

To salvation, He will take me.

Only the Lord is God!

His benignity endures forever.

The Lord is so good,

Even the poor sinner, He has mercy.

To eternal salvation, He will take him.

Work Blessed by God

Oh, God! We cannot do anything,
And if we can do something,
It was thanks to your permission and goodwill.
Only God knows the best for our living.

We must give glory to you before doing something.
For the Lord blesses what we are doing,
May one good work be accomplished,
Being by God's hand blessed.

Your hand is with us to help us,
Multiplying all good works.
Those that will grow us up,
Then our lives will improve.

The Lord wants to see us improving,
It is enough to obey and trust in Him.
He will make everything for us.
For God's plan to be realized,
Then, with gratitude, we are going to glorify you.

Rescued by the Lord

I thought I lived perfectly,

All was good with abundant prosperity.

But something was very wrong.

I did not have God on my side.

All I had were bad things.

Nothing was correct,

Dirty money has bought everything.

I only thought about the money at that moment.

And I have forgotten the Lord's commandments.

One day, God operated in my favor,

He made me see all that horror.

Even knowing that was wrong,

I did not change immediately. I thought:

"What is wrong?

If I do it, it is because I had many losses."

For God, it does not work like that!

One day, finally, I got out of there.

I supposed it would be better.

But I was wrong once more,

And all I made came back against me.

I lost everything I had built.

I was in the deepest pit.

I looked on high, and I asked for forgiveness from God.

I had faith He would find something good in me.

He came and forgave me,

I have passed through tests and tribulations,

After all of it, God lifted me.

Now, I always kept adoring Him.

I trust Him without any doubt.

I know He can change everything.

And each life, He can fix.

Test From God

I always tried to do my best,

To be a good person fearing God.

One day something happened,

And bad things occurred.

I practically lost all I had,

In the blink of an eye, my life was very bad.

I could not understand the reason for it,

I only see all my dreams were destroyed.

I asked God:

"Why, Lord, that happened to me?"

I am yours and fear Thee.

Soon came the answer:

"You know the cause, my son."

I knew the reason for everything.

Because with God and the world, I have been.

That was my test; my tribulation.

The Lord had my heart under evaluation.

Even if knowing everything came from the Lord,

It was not easy to bear.

Many times, I cried a lot,

My voice, I wanted to the Lord hear.

God always answered me:

"Calm down, son, the great day, you will reach."

My anguish grows while I am waiting,

I cried more, and the time was passing.

At the right time, everything fixes it,

All anguishes have been healed by the Lord's hand.

He is our Lord, as it is in his commandment.

From evils, He rid me, great was the assistance.

Now, I only want to adore Him,

Seeking Him each time more.

Then, more He can bless me,

And to eternal life, He will take me.

The Reward for Each One

Sometimes, it seems everything is reversed,
The one who does everything right has difficulties.
The one who does everything wrong has facilities.
The world seems to be upside down.

The correct one was disappointed when he saw this,
They think, *How does God allow happening these things?*
Why does He allow the righteous to be in suffering?
And those who sin are always getting richer.

Do not worry, because God knows everything.
The whole world, He is controlling.
Even if you think there are absurd things.
God has a perfect plan for everything.

Do not question God why the world is like that!
He is the Lord Almighty!
And He must not explain for you or me!
He knows everything, and the wicked will have his end.
Be sure that it will be painful.

What is the use of the wicked to gain everything?

If for the punishment, their soul is going.

He walked away from God and did not know about Him.

Now, at the end of life, it only remains to perish forever.

The Lord sees the suffering of the righteous,

And He satisfies every need.

But many times, we want more,

Do not for need, but only for our vanity.

God gives what He knows will not prejudice us.

There is no use having everything desired for us,

And the heart turns away from the Lord.

Then, our pride will condemn our souls.

For the righteous and faithful is prepared a recognition,

Having a life with plenitude and peace,

To die peacefully and go to eternal salvation.

The Glory of God

Lord, each day, I can see your glory,

I wake up every day with peace and disposition.

Each new day, I live with happiness.

I see your glory when I look to the sky,

Seeing the stars, the moon, and the sun,

Everything was created by the Lord,

To be for us like a headlight.

I can see your glory looking at the sea,

How immense he is!

How many creatures are in its depths!

Under the water, there are too many beauties.

I see your glory when I look at some works,

Because everything created was inspired by the Lord,

The human being is only the constructor.

Lord, I see your glory in the whole world,

Everything you did is so perfect!

Everything is in the right order.

Only the marvelous God can do everything,

He has many sons, and He is a great and eternal father.

Sons on which the Lord has much love.

Giving us all we need,

Preparing us for the greatest glory,

When the eternal life, He will give,

Where we will live to glory and adore Him.

Praise God

Lord, it is so good to sing praises to you,

They are one prayer for my soul.

With praises, I can declare my love for the Lord,

And I also meditate, having peace and calm.

The praise is a pure prayer,

It is a love declaration.

It is marvelous because it comes from the heart.

Making me stay in the spirit of adoration.

I adore you with my lips,

I confess to you all my gratefulness.

I remember all your blessings,

I found compassion, and I have happiness.

Only to the true God, I always will praise,

The Lord is worthy of all my honor and praise,

Because the Lord has loved me first,

From eternal death, He saved me.

I am always praising and hoping for you,

I wait for the day when you will come back and get me,

To the life of eternal peace will lead me,

In your Holy temple, forever, I will praise and glorify you.

The Forgiveness of God

Lord God, forgive my sins,

I am a poor little sinner.

I need you because I am weak.

Forgive me for the mistakes I made.

May your mercy be with me,

Erasing my mistakes and transgressions,

Lord, protect me from the accusations of the enemy,

Because he wants to destroy me with his oppressions.

Lord, remember of my good heart,

May my good days be pleasant to the Lord.

Your forgiveness will be an alliance with me.

Your benignity forever is with me.

Heal me of all impurity and badness,

May, in your paths, I continue walking.

To find true peace and happiness,

And that I can live in your heavenly dwelling.

The Birth

Two thousand years ago, something very special happened,

In a small town, Bethlehem, a child was born.

It was not a usual birth,

It was the greatest event in the history of the Earth.

One new star came to enlighten the world.

It was Jesus Christ, our Lord.

He came to teach us the truth.

The truth is that only He can save us!

God has sent Him to free us.

We are freed from eternal death through Jesus,

He forgives all our transgressions,

Then, with God, we have a true connection.

All praise and glory be given to the Lord,

Even though we are flawed, He loved us.

Giving his only son to rescue us,

He has paid a very high price,

To do the will of the Father.

Confidence in the Lord

Sometimes, I am mocked,

They call me crazy, fanatic, and idiot.

I do not care about this.

Because with the Lord, I have a compromise.

I owe my praise and glory to God,

Only Him is my unique Lord.

To Him, I give all my cry and love,

I trust in his providence and favor.

I follow happy in the path of God,

I obey his commandments and laws.

I am always trying to please Him.

I am waiting for the return of the King of kings.

Jesus! He will come to save us.

I love you, my Lord!

I hope for the promised return.

Lead me until the day arrives,

Because, against me, many people will fight.

The Greatest Sacrifice

Oh Lord, how can I please you?

For you to approve me, what can I do?

Some financial sacrifices, I can do,

But what can I give for who is God and has everything?

There is a thing very valuable that I can give,

My heart, I can give to Thee,

Obeying your laws and decrees.

Keeping my heart sincere and pure.

In my life, forever, the Lord will reign,

Your word will lead me every day.

Then, Lord's favor, I can reach.

And the Lord will bless me.

God! Your grace is marvelous!

With the Lord, my life is glorious.

Your blessings are always with me.

Thank you, Lord, for your mercy.

Thank you for being my best friend.

God's Mercy

Lord God, come to help me!

I am in anguish, and I am very weak,

I need your great favor.

Show me your great love.

There are so many things arising against me.

It seems I have no choice or exit.

That seems to be my end.

Oh Lord, help me quickly!

In your mercy and godliness, I will always trust.

The Lord is the God who makes impossible things,

The One who can change everything.

Only your hand can help me.

Oh Lord, hear my weep and clamor!

And manifest in me your favor.

Your help is my greatest reward.

And this help comes especially,

It comes immensely over me.

Following the Will of God

What is my life on the Earth?
It is just a little steam that soon disperses.
I cannot exalt myself and my plans.
I cannot trust my own hands.

I must trust only in the Lord.
He can do everything.
He is the One who grows my work.
Only the marvelous God can move the world.

Your hands are over all the Earth,
The Lord is the One who rules everything.
Your eyes contemplate my walking,
If I do something according to your will,
The Lord makes my plan prosper.

In this way, I keep my planning,
Always thinking, *If the Lord wills and blesses,*
I will do this or that only if He blesses,
It is the confirmation that I make to please Him.
Then, I will prosper in my life and work.

Acknowledgment to God

I praise and thank God every day,

He is my Lord, and He is always protecting me.

He does not allow anything to be lacking.

He is the unique and true God of love.

He loves me as I am, weak and imperfect.

God chose me to be his son.

He took me from a lake with mud and dirt,

And He put me in rectitude, in righteous ways.

He analyses my walking,

Lead my steps to a wide and spacious place.

One place where there are delights and joyful,

It is a blessed place where reigns the truth.

Lord, keep me in your good way,

Rid me from the evils that pursue me.

Fight against those who seek my end, the enemies,

Bless me always, and may your hand always stay close to me.

The Word of God

Oh, Lord! Your word, I must obey,

All your judgments are wise.

Your statutes are very nice.

Your word is pleasing for your lives.

Only your infinite wisdom can lead us,

Your precepts are perfect for us,

May, in peace, we keep walking.

And from the evil, we can deviate.

Lord, give us a good understanding,

Then, we will look better at your law,

To follow your true commandment,

We will have wisdom, peace, and discernment.

Lord, I thank you for the direction you give us.

One way of light, life, and truth.

The path to save our souls.

Praise God

We should always praise the Lord,

We should always praise with much love.

With many instruments and our voices.

The praise must be pure and from the heart,

God will gladly receive the praise.

All blessings of our God we have to proclaim,

All the wonders He does, we have to sing.

We will proclaim how good it is to follow Him.

Saying how good is to be his son.

We are praising with lovely and pleasant songs.

We are a chosen and holy people,

The Lord took us as sons.

Let us sing this for all nations.

For our God to be praised.

Lord God, it is marvelous to praise Thee.

Father, put a new song on me.

May, I can praise you every day,

And may I always exalt your Holy Name.

The Care of God

There is no evil where the Lord God is.

From all kinds of evils, He freed me,

Your hand is powerful to save,

His children, He will always keep safe.

The Lord loves all his children,

He never forgets or forsakes them.

God supplies all his beloved ones.

They are safe under his protection.

The protection of God is powerful.

He leads the steps and paths of each one.

He does not allow the damage to his faithful one.

He leads him to be saved.

Salvation is not only for Earth's time,

It is salvation for eternal life.

Where everyone will always be with the Lord.

Enjoying the most perfect love.

The Wisdom of God

The Lord knows all things,

Only to you belongs the true knowledge.

Your intelligence is huge and infinite,

In all your works, they inhabit.

Your works are marvelous,

Your works are glorious.

Very perfect is your planning.

All things are ruled by your sovereign knowing,

The Lord orders everything.

Your ordinance is permanent.

Your execution is faithful and trustworthy.

When I see the conclusion of your plan,

I see you are a wise Father and very pleasant.

How great is your wisdom,

The Lord has all knowledge,

Lord, give me a good understanding,

Because this will be amazing for me.

The Work of God on Me

Lord, I love your corrections.

Like a good father, the Lord rebukes me.

I understand that it is not to prejudice me.

It is to make a new heart in me.

My character is modeled by the Lord,

Your hand comes and models my being.

Like a vase, I am being modeled.

In your hands, I always feel beloved.

My shape has already changed,

Little by little, the Lord has transformed me.

He took me out of that old clay,

He is doing me a valuable and honorable vase.

May your hand be always with me,

May my heart always find shelter on Thee.

Because now I am a new creature.

And I want to be always with the Lord.

Gratitude to God

Lord, thank you for my possessions,

I give glory to you for all I have.

The Lord provides everything I need,

Of all confusions, He also rids me.

Precious is all things given by the Lord,

Because He gives with much love.

May I always find grace in your eyes,

And the Lord always improves my life.

May my life be in the center of your will,

May I have a good and generous heart with everyone,

Then kindness will reign in my life.

The goodness is pleasant to the Lord,

Because He is a God with much love.

For everything He does, I will always exalt you,

If I have something, it comes from you.

Daily Protection

Lord, bless my day,

Bless and lead my way,

From all evils that arise,

The Lord will protect me.

Every day, I will face many things,

Some people can arise against me.

Malign traps are trying to catch me,

Destructive bonds are trying to pick me,

Amid all this, there is God to rid me.

He is the Lord God, the Almighty!

Only He can protect me,

He will not allow something to beat me.

God does not allow evil to win.

He will rid me of all evil,

God is the best, and there is no equal!

Because in my life, He will always save me,

And to eternal life, He will take me.

The Plan of God

Apply your will in my life,

I want the Lord to do on me his desire,

Because only the Lord knows the best for me.

All my days, I desire the Lord to lead me.

Only your will is right and perfect,

Your ways are wide and spacious,

The Lord leads to good places,

There are places excellent and marvelous.

Lord, do not let me get discouraged,

Give me strength and hold my hand.

There are many troubles and afflictions,

And there are great tribulations.

I fully trust in the Lord,

Protect me in anguish's day and hear my voice.

Give me strength to always continue,

I desire to be submissive to your will and glorify you.

God, I wait for your will,

I know when you act, it will be a supernatural thing,

Your great glory and power, I will see.

Your great blessing, I will receive.

The Week

Sunday, I go to church,

I seek God with all my heart,

With many songs and praise.

I come back home feeling curated.

I feel renewed, and the Lord gave me strength.

Monday comes and arrives the hardness,

I think, *Oh Lord, what a sadness!*

Soon, God touched my ways.

And He took my weakness far away.

On Tuesday gets close temptation.

Many things are appearing in my life,

They are trying to deviate me from the blessing.

Only God can rid me of that situation.

Wednesday is coming!

The troubles are not stopping.

Only God can rid me.

I am praying for Him to rescue me.

It is already Thursday, and it is almost ending,

The week, the patience, the peace and tranquility.

Only the fights are not ending.

I try to follow firm and strong,

Because the week is going on.

Thank you, God, it is already Friday,

I will go to church today.

I will pray a lot on this day,

I need to be renovated,

Because the week wore me out.

Finally, it is Saturday, a resting day,

I will be renovated on this day,

Tomorrow is Sunday, and one new week will start.

With new challenges and fights.

But I will not stop,

I know I have the company of God.

And from evils, He will save me.

False Gods

People insist on adoring many things,

It can be an image or another thing...

They adore uselessly because there is no power in them.

The images have a mouth and cannot speak,

Ears and cannot hear.

Nor one living spirit to answer.

They always stay stopped, and there is no life in them.

They are works of sinner men,

They do it only to multiply worshipers,

In stone, metal, or wood,

They are made to multiply what is not good.

Because there is only one that we have to adore:

The Lord God!

He can hear our clamor,

We have to pray only to Him.

Only the Lord Almighty can change everything.

Do not seek gods made by humans,

They are bad works of mundane people.

They are an abomination to the true Lord,

He desires our pure praise and love.

Praise only the true God,

He will never forsake us,

Only He can save you, and to eternal life, He will take us.

Wait on the Lord

The Lord acts in mysterious ways,

He does things we cannot understand.

But in the opportune time, his glory will appear.

Showing everyone his powerful hand.

The hand of God comes to help us,

Not in the time we want.

In the perfect time of God, she will come over us.

At the moment that God has prepared for us.

It is not easy to wait for the Lord,

Because we are weak and do not resist the pain.

Even with the pain, we need to have a lot of faith.

We have a God who can do everything!

And to help us, the Lord will never be late.

Trust in the ways of the God Almighty,

All evils will be undone by Him,

Of many ties and curses, we are free.

When you feel alone, pray with the heart,

The Lord will hear your affliction.

He will give you the strength to deal with the situation.

Do not be discouraged, and stay firm in the eternal rock.

When we are in big fights,

It is a signal of victory in our lives.

Spreading Out the Good News

Go into the world and preach the good news.

That is the instruction given by Jesus,

He is the good news that God promised.

We must take this to the world.

So that, they may remember the lamb that perished.

He died to save all people,

So, we have the chance to renew,

Of all sin, He cleanses us.

With a new life in Christ Jesus,

We have to spread his salvation to the world.

Many people are lost and without direction.

They need a word of love and compassion.

Something true that touches the heart.

The gospel of Christ has this power.

The power for everyone to free themselves,

Power for everyone to cure themselves.

For people to know about Jesus,

Only depends on me and you.

We need to spread the message,

Then, in Christ, many people will believe.

They will be free from a world of suffering,

To the protection of God, they are going.

Now, we know what we have to do:

Go to the whole world and announce Jesus,

Giving testimony about cross sacrifice.

Rescuing people from darkness to light.

In this way, the whole world will change.

Rescuing the souls who are lost.

Then, many lives will be saved,

In eternity, together, we will stay.

Path With the Lord

The Lord considers us as a people selected,
Of the rest of the world, we are separated.
To be his children, He took us,
And He is always walking with us.

With us is your mighty hand.
With his mighty arm, He rid us of desolation.
Ridding us of those who rise against, the enemies.
The Lord gives us a safe refuge.

To have all this, He only asks a thing:
"May we love Him with all our hearts,
Moving away from the world's wickedness,
And from all kinds of ungodliness."

Even though God demands so little from us,
Some people cannot obey Him.
They follow in their manner,
About the Lord, they do not matter.

They practice all kinds of bad things:

Idolatry, fights, prostitution, and conflicts.

The Lord gets very sad about it,

He does not like to see his sons doing it.

With them, God does not want to be irate,

He hopes the lost people get to regret it.

With opened arms, the Lord is waiting,

Like a good father, He is forgiving.

The regret must be from the heart,

Then, God gives true forgiveness.

The people who were lost will reconcile with God,

One new life will begin, full of the grace of the Lord.

With peace, praise, and glory.

Because it is the beginning of a new and happier story.

The Coming of the Savior

In ancient times, many people waited for the promised one.

That one would be the Savior, the chosen one.

They knew that something good would happen,

In this world, a new light would come.

It would be someone full of His Holy Spirit,

All it was written, He would accomplish.

Many people would be freed by this man,

Many nations would be saved by this man.

The Jews knew from where He would come,

But they did not know when the promise would be made.

All of them were anxious and with big desire,

They waited for the Messiah in front of their sight.

At the right time, He came to this world,

He was not born wealthy but in poverty.

Because of this, many did not accept Him,

Because they hoped that He would be born as a king.

Among the men, He was despised,

Even so, He has preached the truth of God,

Everyone heard the message and called Him crazy.

"He is demon-possessed," They dared to say.

Jesus did not matter about it,

His way, He followed normally.

He taught everywhere about the Kingdom of Heaven.

Many people were cured.

He was the one and only Son of God,

The Lord sent Him to rescue the world.

But the "Law's masters" did not want to believe.

The Lord Jesus did not give up,

In his mission, He continued.

He left the message of the greatest love,

One love coming from our Lord,

Who sent Jesus to save us,

Of all sins, He can forgive us.

To eternal life on the Father's side, He will take us.

Life With the Lord

The Lord never leaves us.

He is always on our side.

Even when we are misguided,

He never gets out of our life.

God expects us to regret,

In our change, He has pleasure.

Because the Lord does not want to condemn.

Our life and soul, He wants to redeem.

His salvation is something amazing,

In our lives, God is always caring,

He will put us in good places,

Through our lives, we can glorify and exalt Him.

God blessed each life,

For too many people, we will testify.

And seeing the glory of God in our lives,

They may repent and change.

They will come to God, our Savior and Lord,

Everyone, He has loved first.

For a long time, He protected us,

So that we could convert ourselves,

And for everyone, his love, we can declare.

The Late Wrath

Israel and Judah for a long time were sinning.

They did not obey your voice and commandments,

They moved away from you, Lord, going in bad ways,

They burned incense in high places, and for idols, they were curving.

They forgot of all your blessings.

Contaminating themselves with the things of foreign nations.

The people of God joined them in abominations.

They made everything that seemed good in their imaginations.

The Lord has observed all this,

He waited a lot until He got angry.

Even angry, He did not destroy them immediately.

He sent prophets who warned them about their sins.

However, no one wanted to hear them,

Instead, they seek the Lord's servants to destroy them.

The Lord God noticed the people were foolish,

And no one sought to regret the sins.

For a bit more, God held his anger,

Ridding people from the oppressor and thief.

He had hope that the people could change,

And to his presence, they come back again.

Unfortunately, the change never happened,

The whole sinner nation has perished.

Some were killed, and others were taken into captivity.

There, they stayed sad and devastated.

The severity of their sins, they comprehended.

Finding the Way Again

The people insist on not hearing you.

They walk in their own way.

They seek many things, but all are futile.

In the end, they are always lonely.

They wander and miss themselves in their walking,

Because there is no one guiding.

Then, they follow in unpleasant ways,

Choosing detestable things every day.

This wandering life may change,

To the Lord God, you have to surrender.

He will forgive past mistakes,

With God, you will have fresh ways.

You will never stay lonely.

You will stay in good company.

Our celestial Father will guide you.

One good path, you will do.

It will be paths and blessed places.

You will be led to a high place.

To the eternal dwelling place with the Lord.

He rid you of a world very sad.

And forever, your soul, He has saved.

Time of Devastation

There are moments when we are devastated,

All our pillars were destroyed.

Our house seems to be destroyed.

Our structures were unsettled.

We were expelled from our land,

To the captivity, we were sent.

We were put under great tribulation.

We stay subdued, under heavy oppression.

Our eyes dismantle in crying,

We think, *What did we do wrong for this happening?*

In vain, we spent time questioning,

Because we already know the reason this is occurring.

To our Lord, we were disobeying,

We break his holy alliance.

Wickedness and abominations, we were following.

Before He left us in a tough situation,

He advised us because of his love and consideration.

In many ways, He tried to change us.

God always hoped we could change,

And under his law, we would back again.

The Lord delays being angry.

It has come to us many people in his name,

But we did not want to hear them,

We prefer fake words from people.

Now, we pay dearly for it.

Even with too much horror and desolation,

We have hope in the mercy of the Lord,

We hope in his forgiveness and reconciliation,

Because we know He is a God of love.

Desert and Bonanza

Sometimes, a great desert comes to us,
We see around, and there is no one,
We feel very weak and alone,
We need help from someone.

Someone to hear me, someone to whom I can speak to,
Someone who can help me and be sincere.
We seek this person, but it is not easy to find it.
The situation gets worse, and we began to get desperate.

We are in desperation, and there is no good way.
We suffer more and more, day after day.
I got in anguish, desperate, and concerned.
I seek all sides, and there is no solution.

When everything seemed lost, one light came on.
It came from the high, and my problem was gone.
It was a great miracle of the great God,
In a blink of an eye, it happened.

Now, everything is new and renewed,
I got happier and more carefree.
Because I know the Lord is with me.

Mistakes and Truths

For many people, your word is not respected.

They think the bible was created.

They do not have any reverence for Thee,

They think you are an invention and do not exist.

They seek a way to defame you,

They try to convince people that you are not truthful,

They destroy and burn many Bibles,

They think they have autonomy in their lives.

These unbelievers are mistaken in everything.

They are lost in many sins.

They are mired in the middle of the mire.

In great torments, they can be for a long time.

Because they do not have the love of the Lord,

One love that comforted from all weeping.

With a strong arm, He hugged me.

My life was flooded with his glory.

To the Lord love us, we have to hear Him.

We have to love all his commandments.

And we must get away from absurd, mistakes and sins.

Then, we can be his instruments.

We will be instruments of peace and love.

Taking to everyone the message of the Lord,

That One who gave his life for everyone.

Let everyone can know Him.

From a terrible world, everyone can be free,

And to know an indescribable love.

Moving Away From the Lord

The Lord has separated a nation for himself.
Guiding them with a strong arm,
They were always under his protection.
With the Lord, they had a special connection.

They did not need to work to survive,
To the Lord, they should dedicate their lives.
Many delicious things were conceded,
The bread, the meat, and honey fell from the sky.

Everything was perfect and marvelous,
The Lord provided the supply.
He never left nor abandoned them,
Of many evils, the Lord protected them.
Everyone who rose against them,
It was defeated by the Lord's right hand.

Even with all this, they left the Lord.
Serving foundry images, the foreign gods.
They perverted all your holy ways,
Following a detestable abomination,
Contaminating the heart of the whole nation.

Seeing their children were lost,

The chosen ones were sent by the Lord.

The prophets, they were sent to teach,

And every soul, they should rescue.

They had no use to that nation.

God already knew the people were in an insurrection.

To the voice of his prophets, they gave no attention.

After the Lord sent many announcements,

It came over them the punishment.

They were arrested, and they were suffering,

About their bitter life, they were weeping.

This was the reward for their idolatry,

For a long time, they stayed in captivity.

Like that, a lesson was learned:

To have a good life, obey the Lord.

The Love of God

The Lord loves us,

His goodness is forever with us,

He asks us to be obedient,

And we have to fear his commandments.

We have to listen only to his voice,

Only His Holy Name, we must adore.

He can help us. He is the true God.

From his ways, we must not move away.

Out of his law, there are wrong ways,

There are many transgressions, destruction, and mistakes.

Driving our life into a big mud.

For a big evil, we are being consumed.

When the Lord sees our bad situation,

Like a very loving father, He will show his affection.

He desires our sincere conversion,

He wants to hear us asking for forgiveness,

God loves us and wants to save us!

Repenting from evil and returning to the Lord,

He will receive us with big love,

Then, our sins will be forgiven.

It will erase all mistakes in our lives.

We will come back to have a happy life.

Because God will be again on our side.

The Lord in my Battle

Many enemies want to destroy me,
In other lands, they spread death.
With all their strengths, they came to me.
They were stronger and more numerous.

They planned an attack that would come violently,
They came to my boundary.
Their armies arrived with noise and furor.
They wanted to put me in desolation and horror.

Even with many threats, I have never been concerned,
Because I have the Lord with me.
He is my strength, and I will always trust in Him.
The Lord is stronger than any soldier.

He will fight all my fights,
He will defeat those who rise against me.
God is my guardian and protector,
Of many evils and dangers, He already rid me.
I trust in his love, and I am faithful to Him.

The Lord is Our Shepherd

Previously, we walked dispersed,

We went to all sides, like lost cubs.

We did not have anybody who could guide us,

Nobody would go to rescue us.

There was an uncertain and aimless way,

Many have lost themselves along this way,

On the road, other people lost their lives.

With many losses, many people got dispirited.

We needed someone to guide us,

And when a sheep was lost,

He would seek her with great love,

We needed a Savior, one Lord!

The Lord looked at our needs,

He came as our shepherd.

He gathered us in one place,

We stay there to adore and glorify Him.

He rid us of all threats,

All wolves have been taken away.

When some sheep get away,

The Lord goes to seek her with zeal.

Putting her again in his path,

Cleansing any dirt on his fur.

Thank you, Lord, for herd us.

We give you grace for your big love.

May in your sheep pen we can stay forever.

We know that we are saved only by the great shepherd.

Daniel

Your servant, they threw in a distant land,

He was sent to a place so strange.

There, nobody wanted to help him.

Instead, they planned to prejudice him.

In many ways, they tried to accuse him.

Many times, they tried to kill him.

He was persecuted by everyone,

Because the kings had him as their preferred one.

The king was a sinner and did bad things,

But when he observed his servant's living.

He noticed Daniel was following the true God.

The only one who can do everything is the Lord.

He was saved many times because of his faith,

No matter how hard they tried to kill him,

All the time, the angel of the Lord saved him.

Of all evils, he protected him.

God was faithful to his servant.

Never left him to perish nor be defeated.

With power, God always saved him.

Daniel won over all his enemies.

The Salvation

Think in a new place,

Where there is no sadness and crying.

Neither war nor pain or fights.

It will have only love and peace.

I know, it seems impossible to believe,

But this marvelous place will exist.

And all of us can be there.

The Lord Jesus Christ, you need to accept.

Then, He can save you.

Follow the Lord and love Him deeply.

Believe intensely, and ask him for forgiveness.

Jesus defends you in all situations.

And He takes you to the perfect salvation.

One new time in your life will begin,

Because in salvation, you are living.

All days, Jesus will guide you.

In good paths, He will put you.

From the evils that arise, He will protect you.

After a very blessed life,

One day we will come back to the Lord,

We will return to our celestial dwelling place.

We will live one love, very pure and amazing.

Getting Out of the Path

Many times, we insist on contradicting you.

We do not obey and do not hear you.

We insist on not doing what you command.

Your will, we want to ignore.

We do what we think is pleasant.

We let your law and commandment.

We think it is acceptable to do everything.

But this is a big lie!

One lie of who wants to destroy our life.

He works to keep us away from God,

Then we will be the lost sheep from his flock.

Giving a chance for their wolves to devour us,

To death and destruction, they will take us.

These enemies hate us a lot!

They do not accept we have God's love.

At any cost, they want to destroy us.

Of the glory of God, they want to separate us.

Because of this, it is important to submit to the Lord,

For us, He has unconditional love.

Only Jesus is our Lord and Savior.

Only He can protect us from these evils.

Hear what says the Lord's voice:

"Son, renounce the sin and make a new choice,

Just me, the Lord, can save your life.

The eternal life, I can give you.

Only accept my commandments and love me."

Returning to the Path

The voice of God, we do not want to hear.

We prefer to do what we think is interesting.

We change the focus and plan other things.

We forget God, leaving Him waiting.

The way of the Lord stays as plan "B".

We only want God, if something happens.

We think, *Our lives will never change,*

We want to be disobedient, and all will be the same.

In this lie, you must not believe.

Out of the way of God, you are perishing.

Every moment, the enemy tries to destroy you.

In tenebrous paths, he will put you.

And he will make you think that everything is right.

You cannot see how bad it is, you will be blind.

If you mistake, the Lord immediately will correct you.

Like a good father, He will instruct you.

In your life, the Lord will do a correction.

It can be through a big tribulation,

Then you may change your heart.

God wants to see you change,

In your life, God wants to be in the first place,

He wants you to hear the voice of the Holy Spirit again.

Let Him act, and your life will change.

After God transforms you,

Your life will be firm on his will.

Now, God will guide your walking.

To the Lord, you will always be thankful.

Because He did not let you perish,

He rid you of a sad path.

And your life, He has saved.

The Protection of the Family

The demon wants to destroy families,

He puts many traps in the life of the couple.

He uses a lot of ways to do this.

He attacks with many weapons every day.

Because the family is a project of God.

In our hearts, He put the love.

And the love must be shared.

The couple will always have Christ on his side.

One excellent way can be made with Jesus.

He will protect the family with a powerful shield.

The couple will be happy under a perfect covering.

All traps and temptations will be destroyed.

Deliver your family to the Lord Jesus Christ.

Only He can protect everyone's lives.

All your family, He can save.

Under the light and blessings, everyone will stay.

Freed From Sin

One heavy handcuff was on me,

It was hard to walk with it.

I thought to follow in many ways,

Wherever I walked, it was disturbing me.

It seemed that I was a slave.

But it was not usual slavery.

I was a slave of sin.

My life was corroded by many sins.

My soul seemed to be hurt.

I needed my freedom urgently.

I had to get out of this prison of malignity.

I lived every moment, lamenting.

And every day, there were new sufferings.

One day, my long-awaited freedom came to me

The Lord came to me with the key.

From my prison, He freed me.

For me, a new life started.

Of all wickedness, He rid me.

I live under the protection of the God of love.

That One who rid me of all evils.

With his strong arm, He rescued me.

I will adore only Him,

Because only his mercy could free me.

Jesus, Our Lawyer

Do not judge, or you will be judged.

Do not condemn, or you will be condemned.

Jesus himself did not come to judge us.

The Lord came to save us.

In our case, He will defend.

When the enemy comes against,

Jesus is ready to fight for us.

Of all charges, the Lord will rid us.

The evil of the enemy will be defeated.

With Jesus, a new life you will start.

One excellent protection, you will get.

One thing is necessary for this:

You have to confess Jesus as Lord and Savior.

That one who confesses Jesus will be saved.

For, before God the Father, Jesus will confess us.

Of a terrible destiny, He will rid you.

To eternal life, He will lead you.

Rapture

As a light, it will come on that great day.

Suddenly, it will appear in every place.

Many people will not know what to do.

They will think, *What was it that we saw happen?*

What happened was the return of the Son of God.

Jesus Christ returned and took his people to the Lord.

He took all those that were fair and correct.

In this world, only wicked people, He has left.

Those who stayed will think, *How can it be?*

Without God, in darkness, this world will perish!

That will be the hard and true reality.

The Lord warned everyone about it.

But unfortunately, many people did not want to hear Him.

The people abandoned the word of God.

Everyone preferred to live in their sins.

They got out of right and good ways,

They only remember Christ in suffering days.

Do not let this happen to you.

Do not wait to see and then believe.

Accept Jesus as Lord, and you will not regret it.

The eternal life, He will give you.

Of many torments and tribulations, He will rid you.

The Wonders of Christ

The Lord walked throughout the whole of Israel's land.

Many people were healed by his hands.

The people were cured of all diseases.

Much news about his acts was spreading.

Where He did go, all people recognized Him.

The evil spirits feared Him when He was approaching.

Because they knew the Lord would send them to hell.

The great promise of the Lord was accomplished:

He would rid people of all evils.

Many people were delivered of many evils by his hand.

He cured diseases, cleansed leprosy, and cast out demons.

The one who has this power is Jesus Christ!

Only the Son of God can do all of it!

Besides that, He left a beautiful message.

We have to love each other,

And we have to practice kindness to our brothers.

Then He made clear the purpose of the one who sent Him,

The love of God, He was showing.

He loved us so much that He gave his son.

He was humiliated, and on the cross, He was crucified.

Jesus made all of it for love.

By his sacrifice, we were saved.

He took our sins over himself.

After three days, He resurrected and to heaven, elevated himself.

On the side of God, He will intercede for us forever.

With us, his Holy Spirit is our comforter.

Every day we are watching and waiting.

For the day of the Lord's second coming.

Thank You for Jesus Christ

Our Lord was the saint of Israel.

The Living God, Emmanuel.

You were here with us for a little.

To console us and wipe out our tears.

One new life, you came to introduce us,

Under the covering and blessing of the God of love.

The Lord who wants to save us.

Jesus came to bear our sins.

So, we would have the opportunity to cleanse ourselves.

Our failures and mistakes were put over him.

He took up our pain and suffering.

The glory of God has been revealed in Him.

And most important, He forgave our sins.

God made a new alliance with us.

One everlasting covenant.

Demonstrating that He always will be a God of love.

He has much love for his children.

Paying a high price to save them.

Because on our behalf, Jesus Christ was given.

We had a new opportunity to live.

The hope of eternal life, we have come to know.

Thank you, Lord, for doing it.

Thank you, God, for sending your Son.

The Grace of Salvation

When a sinner repents,

Changing his life and obeying the Lord,

The hell shakes! Because a slave was freed.

Now, he will live a new life with love.

He will love the one who saved him,

He was taken from one stinky mire.

His face was wiped of all weeping.

From now on, he will be full of happiness,

Because he is following the true path.

He is on the side of the Lord.

He left Satan and his horde.

Over his life, the demon has no control.

Day and night, he is protected by the Lord's angels.

Everything he does will be for the Lord.

Demonstrating his gratitude and love.

He will praise only the powerful God.

He will never forget the day he was saved by God.

The love of God is amazing.

From death to eternal life, God has taken him.

Back to the Gospel

Lord, we always like to ask for everything.

We seek you when we want to get one thing.

We are going to you desiring to be rewarded.

We turn into despicable and unfaithful servants.

Because we forget the Gospel preached for Christ.

Jesus preached salvation and a life with humility.

Instead of a life full of material goods and vanity.

The Holy Gospel came to save our souls.

It did not come to satiate our wishes.

The Lord wants us to adore Him with all our hearts.

God desires we love our brothers.

If the wealth and material goods, we start to desire.

Soon our heart is going to be contaminated,

The words of God, he will forget.

Every day, we have to consult the Gospel.

In our lives, the teachings, we have to apply.

On it is contained the key to saving our lives.

If this is not made, we are negating Christ.

We will negate his teaching and sacrifice.

too late to go back to the Gospel.

We have not to be enchanted with material goods.

Let us look to the grace of salvation.

This is the best gift that God could give us.

Jesus, the Good Shepherd

Lord Jesus, you have been since the beginning.

He has been with God since the origin.

He participated in all creation.

Everything He made is a powerful demonstration.

His hand has the power to gather his sheep.

Of all places, they have been gathered,

In a unique place, they have been put,

Inside a very good sheepfold,

Because the Lord is a shepherd very zealous.

The zeal to protect his sheep.

He does not allow anyone to be lost.

How the Lord is a good shepherd!

He rid them of the destructor.

For his sheep, He has a big love.

He loved them so and delivered himself for them.

He suffered for each one of them.

He did everything to protect the sheep.

Ridding them of the one who wants to kill and spread.

To save us, Jesus faced everything.

His life, He delivered.

So that the sheep that follow him,

On the last day, they will resurrect.

Something Wrong

I am living, and I feel trapped.

It seems there is something odd in my life.

I feel like something is not right.

It is like I had a load on my back.

One load that disturbs my walking.

Even though I am trying to do my best,

I can never get up.

Talk, Lord, what is wrong in my life!

I need to know what is stopping me!

I need to know what is always arresting me!

God, give me an answer!

Because I want to get out of this lukewarm life.

After asking, God showed me.

It was something that deeply touched me.

Through a beloved pastor,

The great answer of the Lord came to me.

It was something like that:

"My son, I say to you what is wrong.

You say to yourself that you are mine,

But in fact, you live a masked life.

My works, you want to make.

But my law, you do not want to obey.

You live like a double man,

In the church, you are a blessing,

And outside, you are serving the sin.

Living like that, nothing will change.

You have to decide which side will win.

Or you come to me, with fear and uncovered face.

Or then, you stay pretending to be a good man.

And you will burn in hell in the end."

After such a strong word, I decided.

I threw away the mask, and only the Lord, I will serve.

I understood that only He has the best for me.

Until the end, I will stay only with Him.

The Lord's Supper

In your supper, we eat your body,

And we drink your blood.

We have faith in your holy word.

We know that with the Lord,

We have a new chance.

Chance to save our soul,

Opportunity to confess your name.

Because when we eat with the Lord,

We can participate in his body.

The wine is to symbolize your bloodshed.

And to demonstrate your flesh, we have the bread.

When I eat, I say to the world:

"I believe in your great sacrifice!

I believe in your resurrection in the promised time."

Now, the Lord is in me.

On the body of the Lord, I am within.

I feel with new force.

Because I make a new covenant of love.

I am professing my faith in my Savior and Lord.

Jesus resurrected, and He is among us.

Have a better relationship with Him.

In his supper, come to participate.

You will reconcile if you eat faithfully.

In your life, Christ will always stay living.

A Seductive World and the Love of God

The things of the world want to seduce you.

There are beautiful things shown to deceive you.

You think, *How everything is good and marvelous!*

But all is a big trap of the enemy.

Because he wants to destroy you.

The first step is to put you away from the church.

He will show you the beautiful world in every way.

On TV, radio, internet, with friends, or in the street.

To put you away from God, he does everything.

Then, in your life, he will make something.

It will be a strong touch when he touches you.

It is death's touch, what he wants to do.

Little by little, he will addict you to something.

Then, you will lose everyone, and you will be lonely.

One addiction will bring you to another.

When you notice, you seem like a dead body.

Your body will be almost destroyed.

Many times, you ask yourself:

"How can I still be alive yet?"

You are alive because God loved you.

Of death, many times, He rid you.

Because the Lord always believed in you.

He believes one day you will change,

And to his love arms, you would come back again.

With your amazing Father, you will make reconciliation.

God has never abandoned you even in your tribulations!

Even though it seems everything is lost,

Do not give up! You are a son of God.

Repent of all evil wholeheartedly.

The Lord will give you his hand immediately.

He will take you from a deep abyss.

He will put you in a place, new and clean.

God will erase all mistakes and sins.

Then, a new life can begin.

One life of peace with the Lord,

Professing Christ as your unique Savior.

You will always remember from where the Lord has taken you.

Thanking Him every day for his great love.

The Holy Spirit

The Lord rose to heaven after He was resurrected.

His beloved ones were not abandoned.

Because the Holy Spirit stayed with us.

Then, He can console us.

And He always can help us.

The Holy Spirit is a sweet comforter.

And every day, He increases our love.

He will connect our spirits to God.

Then, intensely, we will praise the Lord.

We could know the Holy Spirit.

Then, all the good things of God, we could see.

We could be convinced about the sin.

Because only the love of God has that power.

The Holy Spirit is who transforms us.

Only Him can come and change us.

Because He does not come with reason.

He comes with the love of God directly in the heart.

If you want the Holy Spirit to dwell in you,

One self-purification is what you have to do,

With much fasting, bible, praise, and prayer.

In this way, God will grace you.

And the Holy Spirit will come upon you.

The Temptation and the Protection

I have to sanctify myself every day.

Because every time I wake up,

Soon, the sin comes to tempt.

The evil one wants to put me away,

From the Lord's will and commandments.

The demon uses many people for his purpose,

He even uses close friends,

They say good things.

But they are not saying by themselves,

They are being used by the enemy.

The evil one uses all his might.

He will declare war against my spirit.

In every way, he is trying to cheat me,

Then, before God, he can accuse me.

I know to live in this world seems hard,

But, as I said, I have to seek sanctification.

For it, I have to pray, fast and do Bible meditation.

Running away from evils and temptations.

The Holy Spirit is with me in all situations.

Everything that rises against me will be defeated!

I have God who can protect me.

The strength for winning evils, He gives me.

He sends his angels to cleanse the way.

He never let me be lonely.

May the Lord's hand always be with me,

During good and bad times, He stays here.

May the will of God be done,

And my life is always right.

The Marvelous Salvation

We were saved by the grace of Jesus.

By His love, we were freed of sin.

Now, we have full liberty.

This miracle can be done only by the God Almighty.

It was the miracle of our salvation.

Giving everyone the opportunity to be forgiven.

Ridding the sinner from all condemnation.

God extended his hand to us.

God did not want to see our destruction.

We cannot do anything to be chosen by Him.

It is the Lord who chooses us to convert.

Because in us, He saw a good thing.

He called us to believe in his Son.

We have to repent of all sins.

After repenting and asking for forgiveness,

We will be totally free of slavery.

We will be a tool in the hands of God.

In the life of many people, we will be a fountain of love.

One fountain to announce the blessing of the Lord.

Then, many souls, we will gain,

Many people will be freed of sin.

We will make the will of the Lord.

We will spread the good news to the entire world.

About the author

Rafael Henrique dos Santos Lima

Associate Degree in Administration and M.B.A. in Strategic Project Management by Centro Universitário UNA. Christian by the grace of God. Passionate about writing (English, Portuguese, Spanish), poet and novelist.

Contacts

rafael50001@hotmail.com

rafaelhsts@gmail.com

Blog: escritorrafaellima.blogspot.com

Acknowledgement

The following sites contain a lot of useful information for the translation.

Google Docs

Google Translator

Grammarly

RhymeZone

Oxford Dictionary

Special acknowledgement

I thank God. He gave me the intelligence to write the poems.

www.ingramcontent.com/pod-product-compliance
Lightning Source LLC
Chambersburg PA
CBHW081928120726

47997CB00010B/3077